PIANO Adventures®

SCALE AND CHORD BOOK 3

Harmony in Motion

Randall Faber

Online Support
Visit **pianoadventures.com/scales** to find
online support for this book!

Production Coordinator: Jon Ophoff
Editor: Elizabeth Gutierrez
Engraving: Dovetree Productions, Inc.

FABER
PIANO ADVENTURES®

ISBN 978-1-61677-663-3

Table of Contents

This book develops powerful skills. Work on it diligently with two objectives:

1) To learn essential music theory patterns at the keyboard.

2) To develop technical fluency, including evenness of tone, evenness of rhythm, and eventually speed.

Sections 1 and 2 provide a valuable orientation. While you may have already studied one-octave scales, the exercises in these sections will deepen your understanding. Take your time here and focus on touch and sound, especially the *feel* of the black keys under your hands. Work through the transpositions. These are important and will engage your thinking for better pattern recognition.

As you move through the major keys of Sections 3 and 4, you may concurrently explore the same keys in Section 7 Harmony.

When you are fluent with an exercise, chart your progress through the transpositions. Make notes in your book, including tempo marks that help track your progress.

Celebrate the completion of each unit! These are important milestones for you as a developing musician.

MemoriZe

FF30

Transpose

Black Key Patterns in Sharp Keys

A *scale* reduces 88 keys to seven tones.

The black keys help you to *feel* your way around the keyboard.

Fingers drape over the black keys. The thumb plays on white keys.

Begin with the most comfortable scale, B major, which uses all five black keys.

♩ = 72 to 120

B Major

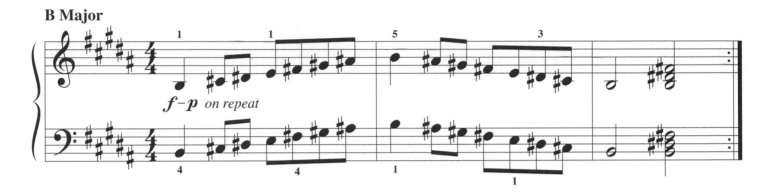

f-*p* on repeat

E Major

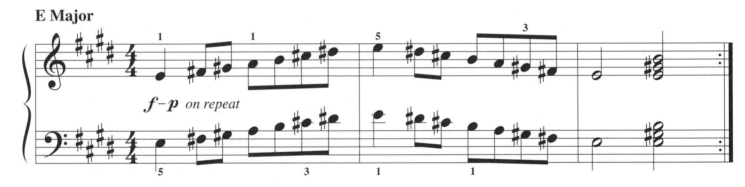

f-*p* on repeat

A Major

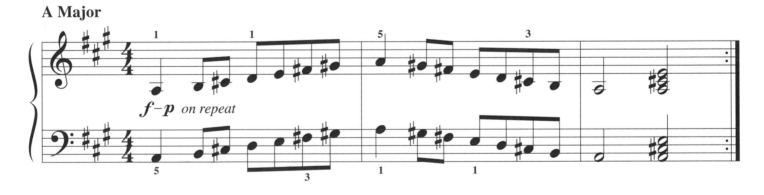

f-*p* on repeat

D Major

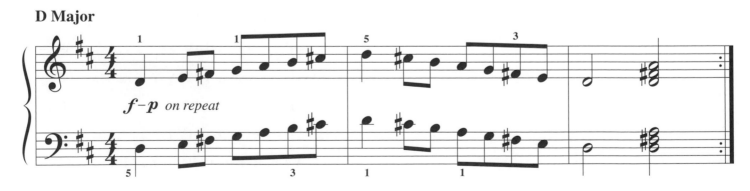

f-*p* on repeat

Note: The keys of F♯ and C♯ major are presented
in Section 2 as G♭ and D♭, respectively.

Continue by transposing to these keys:

G	C

FF30

Sharp Key Signatures

1. For each key signature below, circle the last sharp. Then name the key.
   Hint: the last sharp is the *leading tone* (scale degree 7).

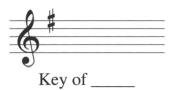

Key of _____

Key of _____

Key of _____

Key of _____

Key of _____

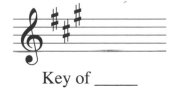

Key of _____

2. For each of the keys indicated, name the *leading tone* (scale degree 7),
   the *tonic* (scale degree 1), and the *dominant* (scale degree 5).

Key of G	
Leading tone:	_____
Tonic:	_____
Dominant:	_____

Key of B	
Leading tone:	_____
Tonic:	_____
Dominant:	_____

Key of A	
Leading tone:	_____
Tonic:	_____
Dominant:	_____

Key of E	
Leading tone:	_____
Tonic:	_____
Dominant:	_____

Key of D	
Leading tone:	_____
Tonic:	_____
Dominant:	_____

Key of C	
Leading tone:	_____
Tonic:	_____
Dominant:	_____

V to I in Sharp Keys

The V harmony is anchored by scale degree 5 in the bass.
Notice how it harmonizes the leading tone and scale degree 2.

What chord is spelled by scale degrees 5, 7, and 2 in the key of C?

Melodic resolution: *leading tone* **to** *tonic* **(scale degree 7 to 1)**

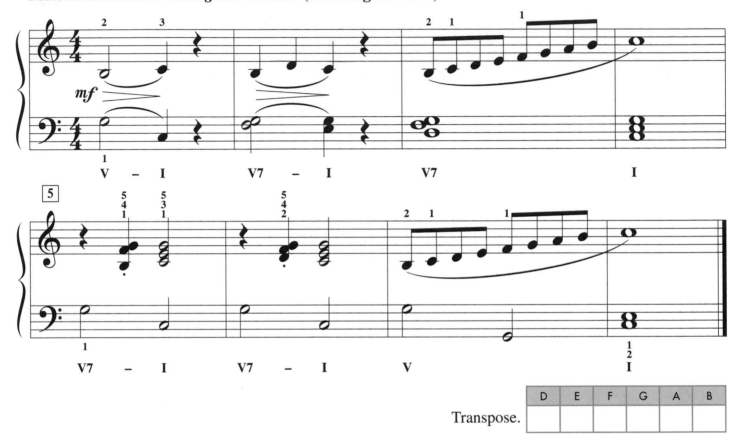

Transpose.

D	E	F	G	A	B

Melodic resolution: scale degree 2 to 1

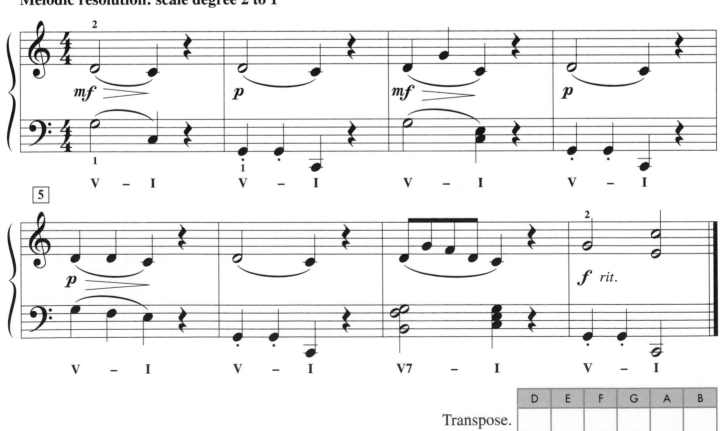

Transpose.

D	E	F	G	A	B

FF302

Circles on Scale Degrees 1 and 5

Use wrist circles[1] to make graceful turns through the 4ths and 5ths.

Lightly *pulse* the first note of each measure with a burst of arm weight.[2]

$\downarrow = 72$ to $\downarrow = 88$

[1] See Piano Adventures® Level 3A Technique & Artistry Book page 36.

[2] Arm weight refers to the use of gravity and relaxation.
    See Piano Adventures® Level 2B Technique & Artistry Book page 2.

Now transpose.

G	D	A	E

Triplet Scales

Notice the emphasis on the leading tone (scale degree 7) and the dominant (scale degree 5).

Transpose.

E	G	A	B

Major 3rd and Tritone

The upper part of a major scale—scale degrees 4 to 7—is comprised of whole steps. Scale degrees 4 and 7 form the unsettled interval of a *tritone*.

Scale degrees 1-3 in a major scale also span whole steps. Listen to the settled sound of this major 3rd (M3), in contrast to the unsettled tritone.

As you play, listen how scale degree 7 leads up by half step to the tonic, and scale degree 4 resolves down a half step to 3.

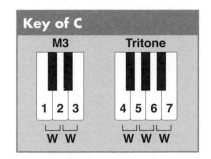

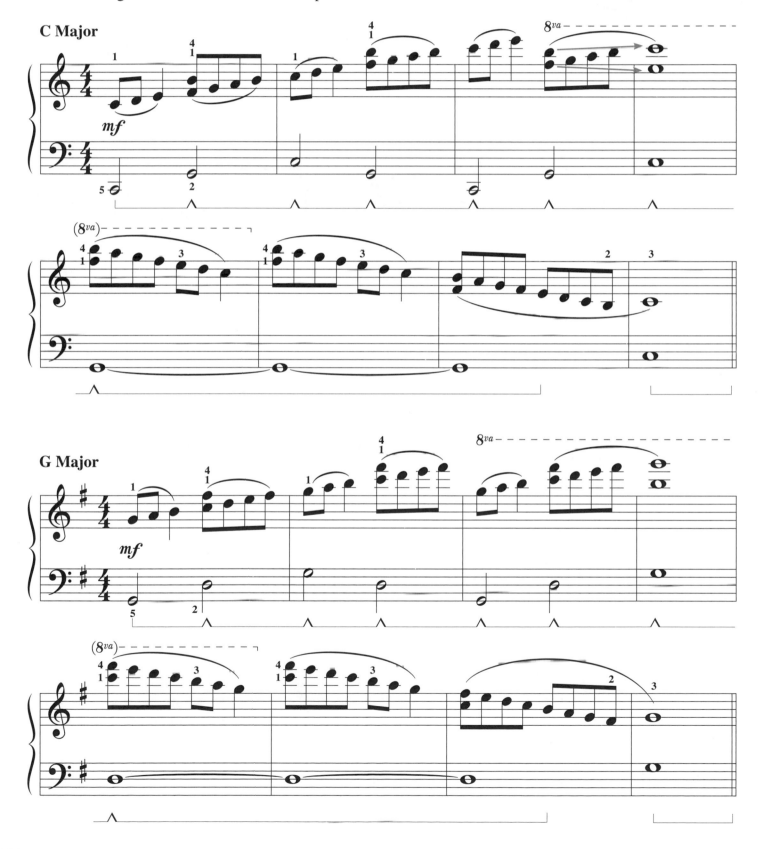

D Major

A Major

FF302

E Major

B Major

Black Key Patterns in Flat Keys

Fingering for Flat Scales

R.H. Thumb plays on the first white key *ascending*.

For the R.H., this is always C and F.

L.H. Thumb plays on the first white key *descending*.

F Major

Notice that the second to last flat in the key signature is the name of the key.

B♭ Major

FF302

E♭ Major

A♭ Major

D♭ Major

G♭ Major

Flat Key Signatures

1. For the key signatures below, circle the next to last flat. Then name the key.

Key of __F__   Key of _____   Key of _____

Key of _____   Key of _____   Key of _____

2. For each of the keys indicated, name the *leading tone* (scale degree 7), the *tonic* (scale degree 1), and the *dominant* (scale degree 5).

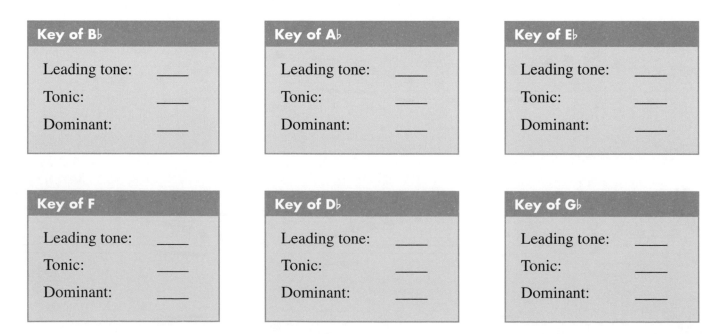

Key of B♭		
Leading tone: ____		
Tonic: ____		
Dominant: ____		

Key of A♭		
Leading tone: ____		
Tonic: ____		
Dominant: ____		

Key of E♭		
Leading tone: ____		
Tonic: ____		
Dominant: ____		

Key of F		
Leading tone: ____		
Tonic: ____		
Dominant: ____		

Key of D♭		
Leading tone: ____		
Tonic: ____		
Dominant: ____		

Key of G♭		
Leading tone: ____		
Tonic: ____		
Dominant: ____		

FF302

V to I in Flat Keys

Melodic resolution: descending 3-2-1

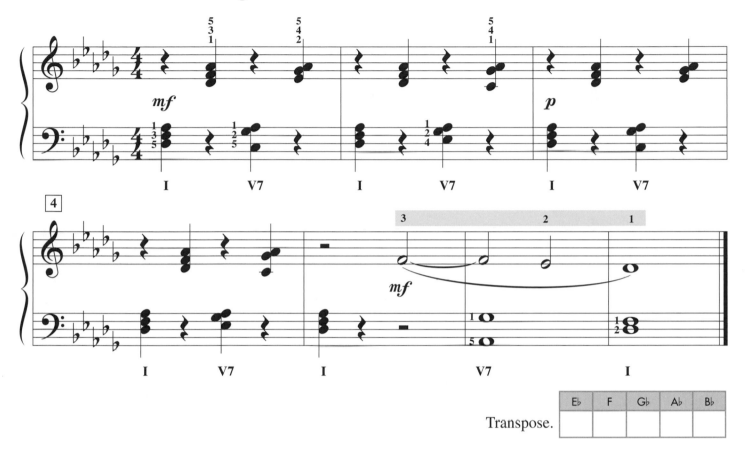

Transpose.

Eb	F	Gb	Ab	Bb

Melodic resolution: *leading tone* **to** *tonic*

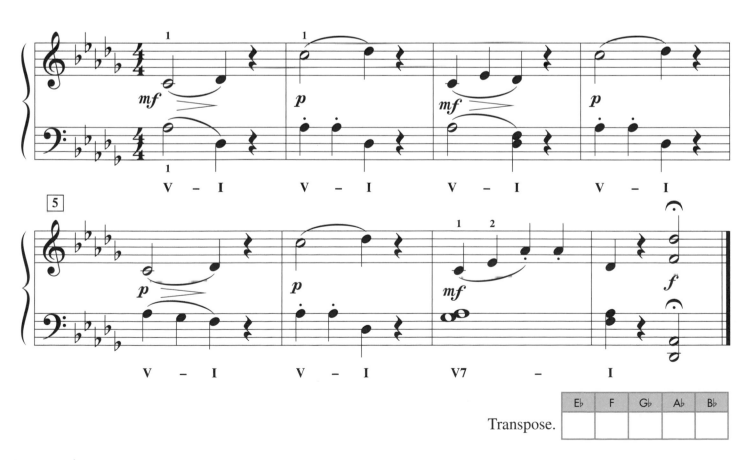

Transpose.

Eb	F	Gb	Ab	Bb

Major 3rd and Tritone

Notice the I harmonization over scale degrees 1-3 and the V7 harmonization for degrees 4-7.

D♭ Major

A♭ Major

FF302

E♭ Major

B♭ Major

Two-Octave Scales

Practice hands separately, listening for evenness of tone and rhythm.
Work up to hands-together playing, practicing the Speed Drills on pages 24-25.

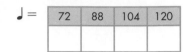

C Major

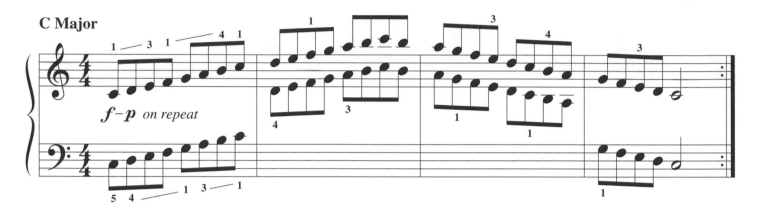

G Major

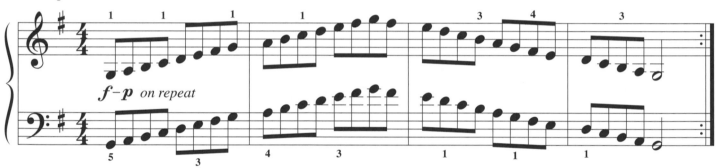

D Major

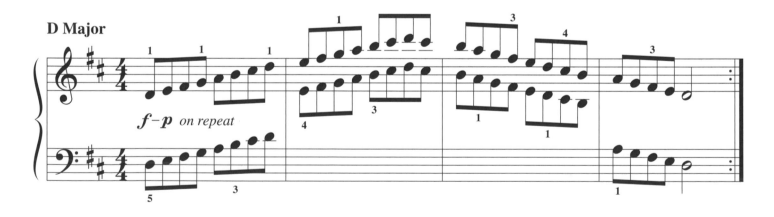

A Major

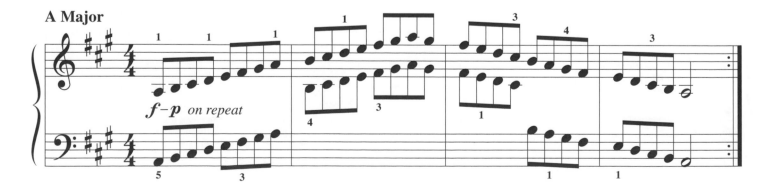

FF302(

E Major

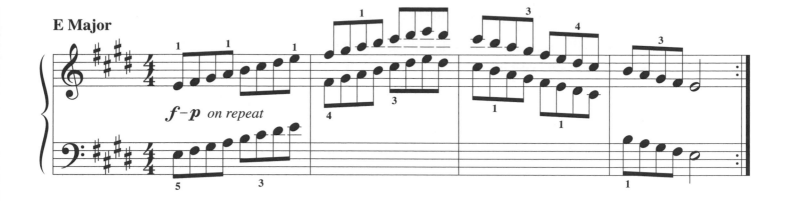

B Major

F♯ Major

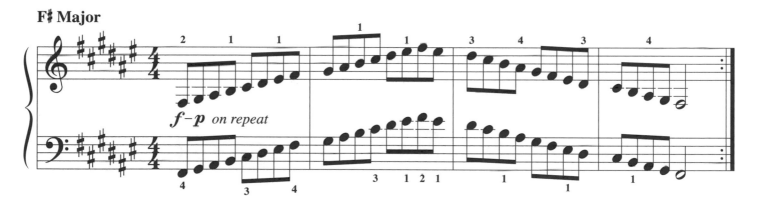

Variation: Contrary Motion

Try playing scales in *contrary motion*.
Notice the matching fingerings between the hands.

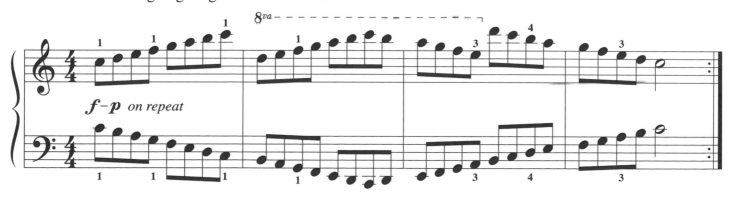

Transpose to all of the above keys.

G	D	A	E	B	F♯

Three-Octave Preps

Three-octave scales are typically practiced in triplets.

♩ = 80 to 112

Notice the scale degree and fingering at each downbeat (first note of a measure).
These descend stepwise.

Here the triplet feel is notated in $\frac{6}{8}$ time (compound meter).

♩. = 80 to 112

What scale degrees are played during the V7?

FF302

Tonic-Dominant Swirls

♩. = 80 to 112

C Major

D Major

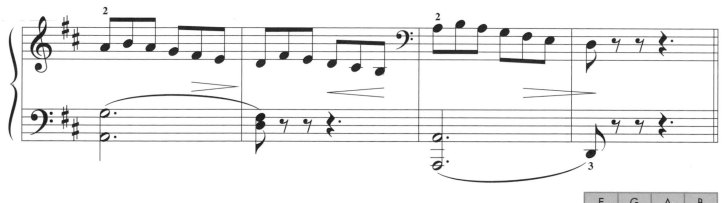

E	G	A	B

Transpose.

Three-Octave Scales

Choose your dynamics.

♩ =	66	72	80	92

C Major

G Major

FF3020

D Major

A Major

Transpose to E and B major using the fingering learned.

E	B

Building Speed in Sharp Keys for L.H.

Alternate measures as **strong** and **weak**.

- Pulse the downbeat of *strong* measures using a drop of arm weight.

- Pulse the downbeat of *weak* measures with an up motion from an active finger and a rising wrist through the measure.

The fingering at each downbeat progresses stepwise: 5, 4, 3.

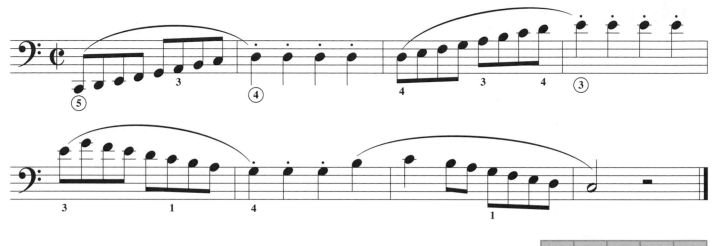

	D	E	F	G	A
Transpose.					

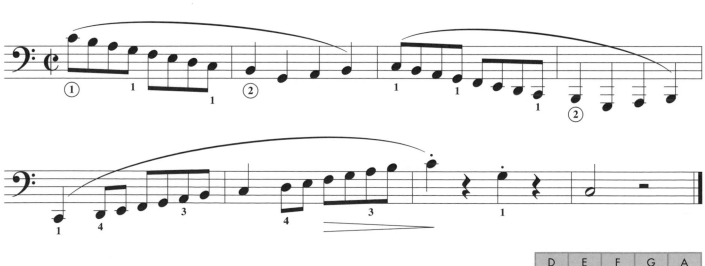

	D	E	F	G	A
Transpose.					

FF302(

Building Speed in Sharp Keys for R.H.

Alternate measures as **strong** and **weak**.

- Pulse the downbeat of *strong* measures using a drop of arm weight.

- Pulse the downbeat of *weak* measures with an up motion from an active finger and a rising wrist through the measure.

$\frac{1}{2} = 72$ to 92

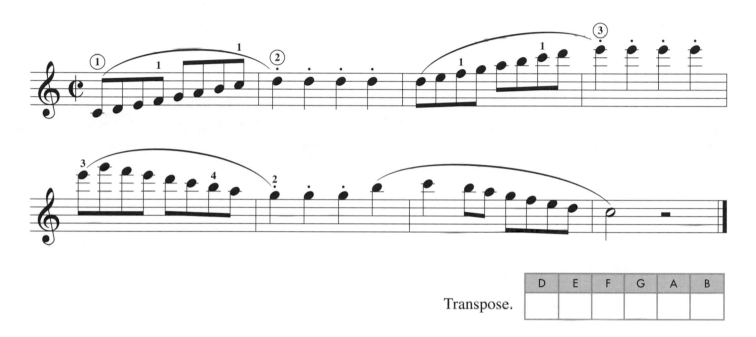

	D	E	F	G	A	B
Transpose.						

Notice the fingering (and scale degree) at each downbeat. The fingering progresses stepwise: 1, 2, 3.

Pulse each of these downbeats. At faster tempi, alternate between downward and upward pulses.

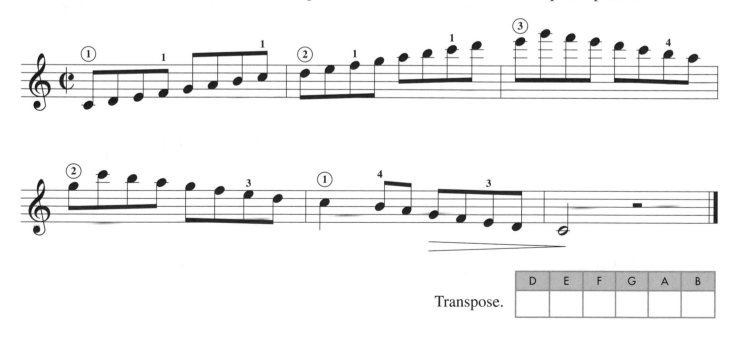

	D	E	F	G	A	B
Transpose.						

Four-Octave Scales for L.H.

Play these scales one octave lower than written.

What do you notice about the circled fingering?

♩ =

72	80	88	96

C Major

G Major

D Major

FF302e

A Major

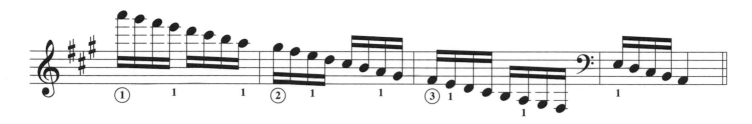

E Major

B Major

Four-Octave Scales for R.H.

Notice how each measure begins on the next scale degree:
1-2-3-4 ascending; 8-7-6-5 descending.

♩ =	72	80	88	96

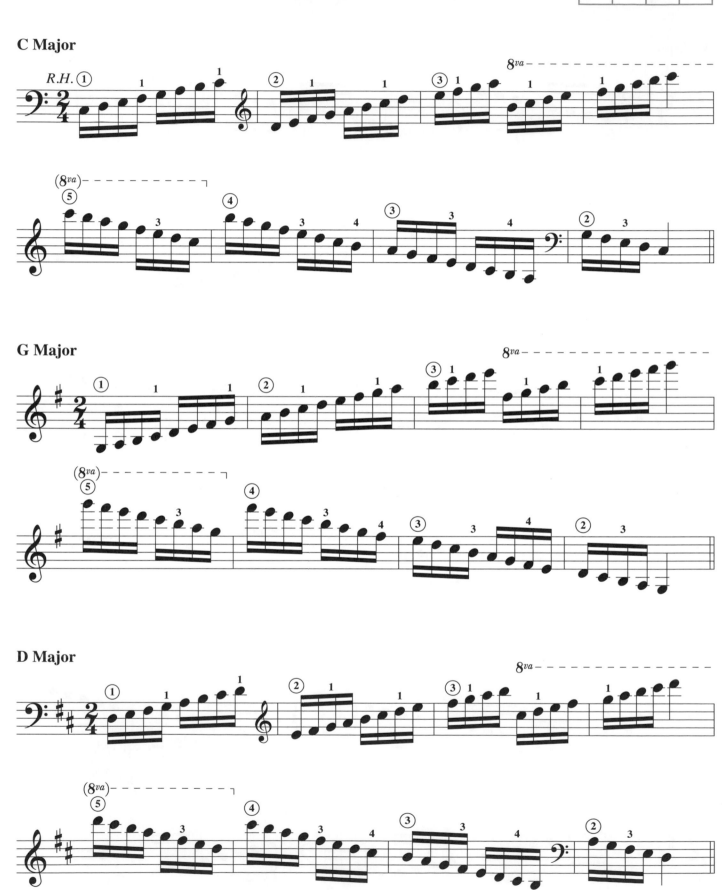

C Major

G Major

D Major

A Major

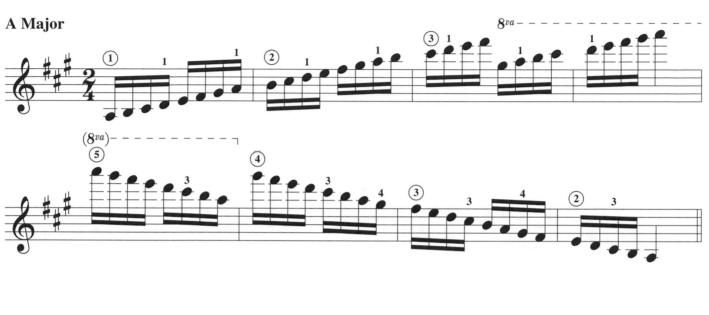

E Major

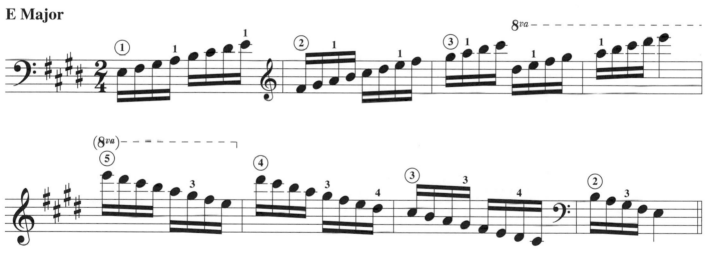

B Major

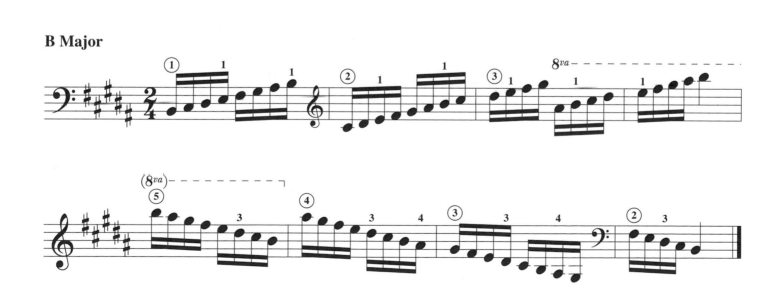

Multi-Octave Major Scales in Flat Keys

Two-Octave Scales

Practice hands separately, listening for evenness of tone and rhythm.
Work up to hands-together playing, practicing the Speed Drills on pages 32-33.

♩ =	72	88	104	120

F Major

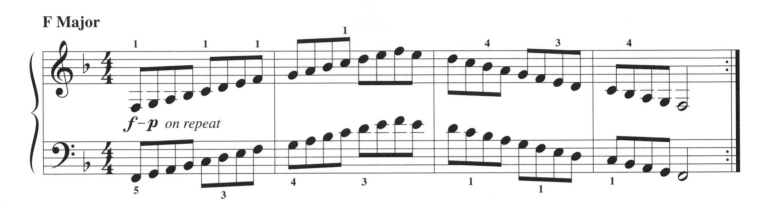

B♭ Major

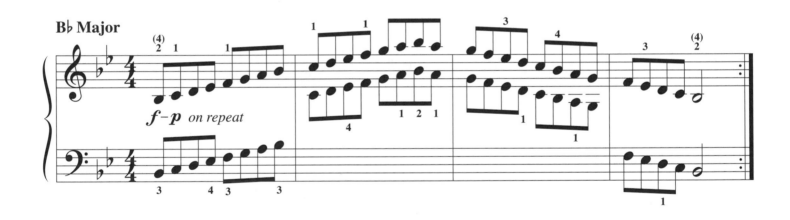

E♭ Major

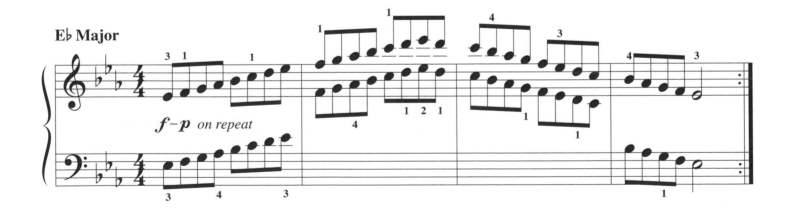

A♭ Major

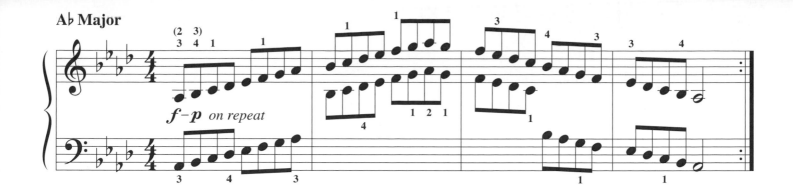

D♭ Major

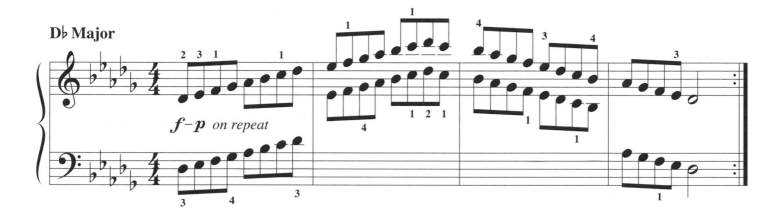

G♭ Major

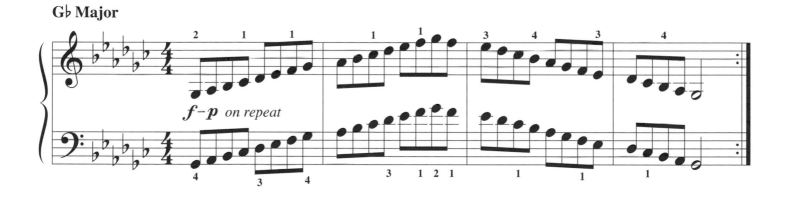

Variation: Parallel 10ths

After learning the above, play this variation in all of the above keys.
Notice the parallel 10ths, followed by parallel 6ths.

♩ = 66 to 100

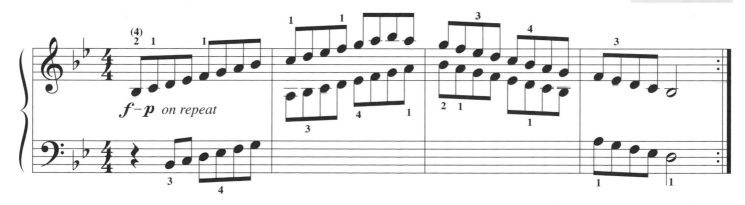

Transpose to all of the above keys.

F	Bb	Eb	Ab	Bb	Gb

Building Speed in Flat Keys

For R.H. flat key scales, the thumb plays on C and F.
The R.H. fingering is consistent: three fingers up from C, and four fingers up from F.

Notice this pattern of
three fingers / four fingers.

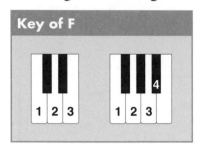

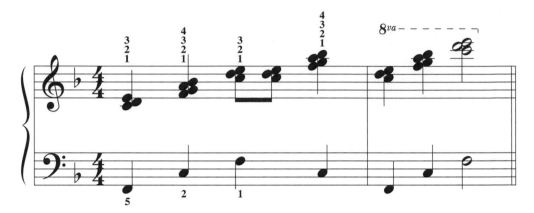

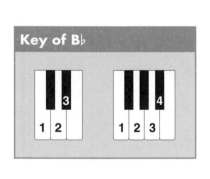

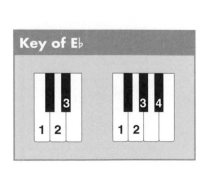

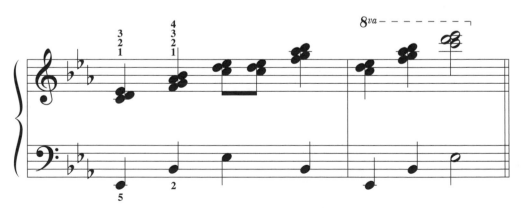

FF3026

Key of A♭

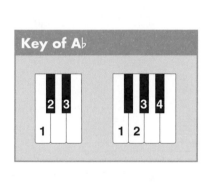

Key of D♭

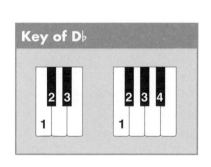

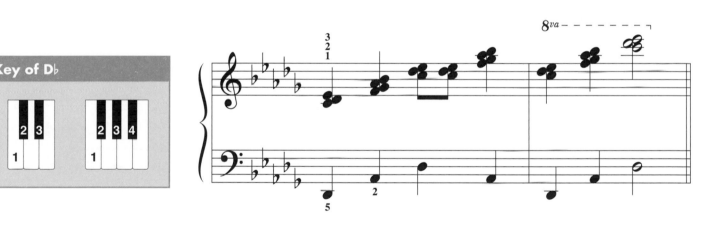

Key of G♭

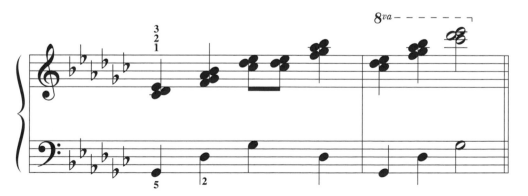

Three-Octave Preps for L.H.

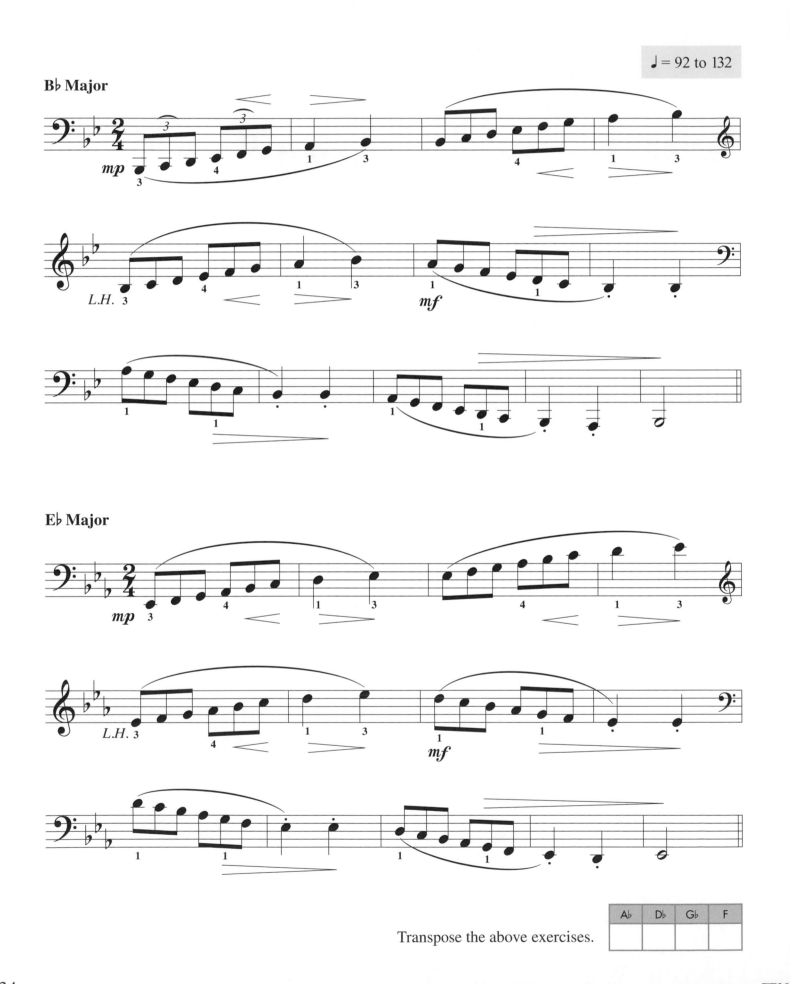

Transpose the above exercises.

A♭	D♭	G♭	F

Three-Octave Preps for R.H.

Transpose the above exercises.

A♭	D♭	G♭	F

Three-Octave Scales

Choose your dynamics.

♩ =	66	72	80	92

F Major

B♭ Major

FF3026

E♭ Major

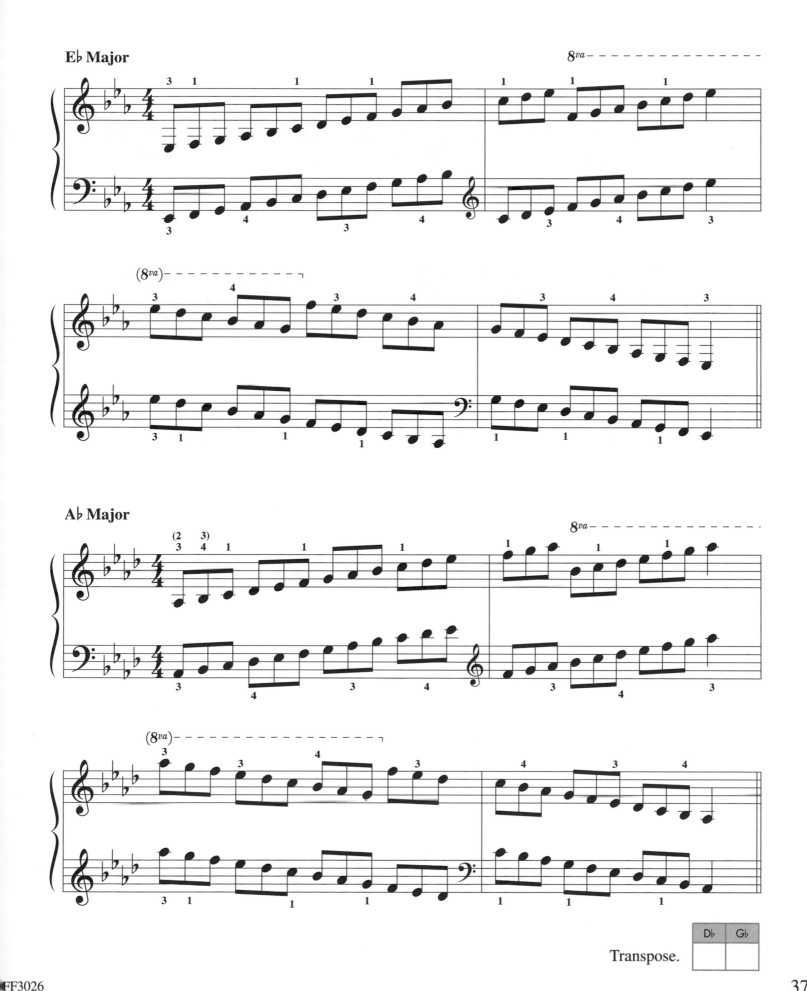

A♭ Major

Transpose.

D♭	G♭

Four-Octave Scales for L.H.

What do you notice about the circled fingering?

♩ =

72	80	88	96

F Major

L.H. ⑤

L.H. ①

B♭ Major

E♭ Major

8va – – – – – – – ⌐

8va – – – – – – – ⌐

A♭ Major

D♭ Major

G♭ Major

Four-Octave Scales for R.H.

What do you notice about the circled fingering?

♩ =	72	80	88	96

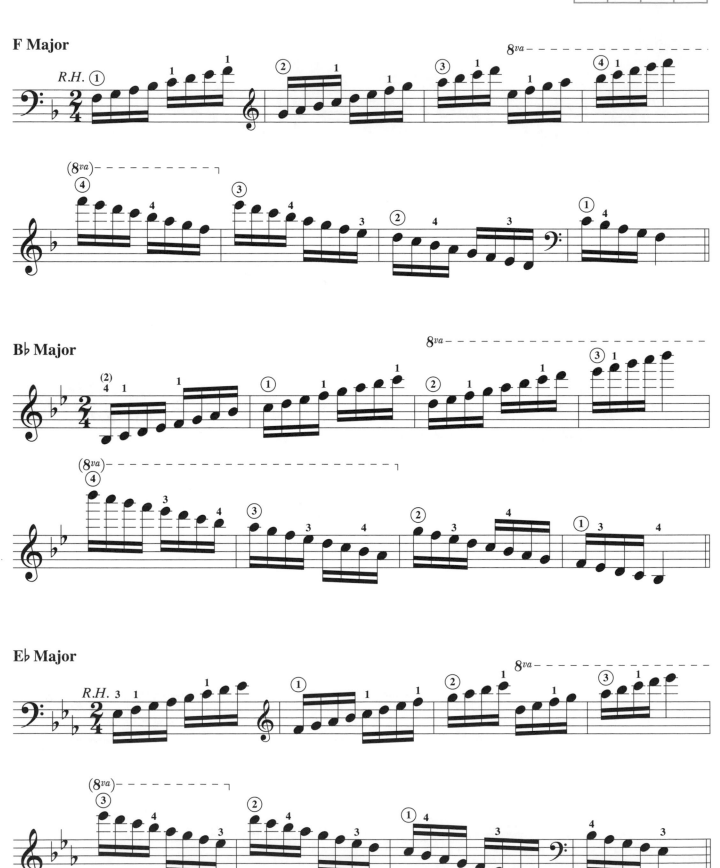

F Major

B♭ Major

E♭ Major

FF302

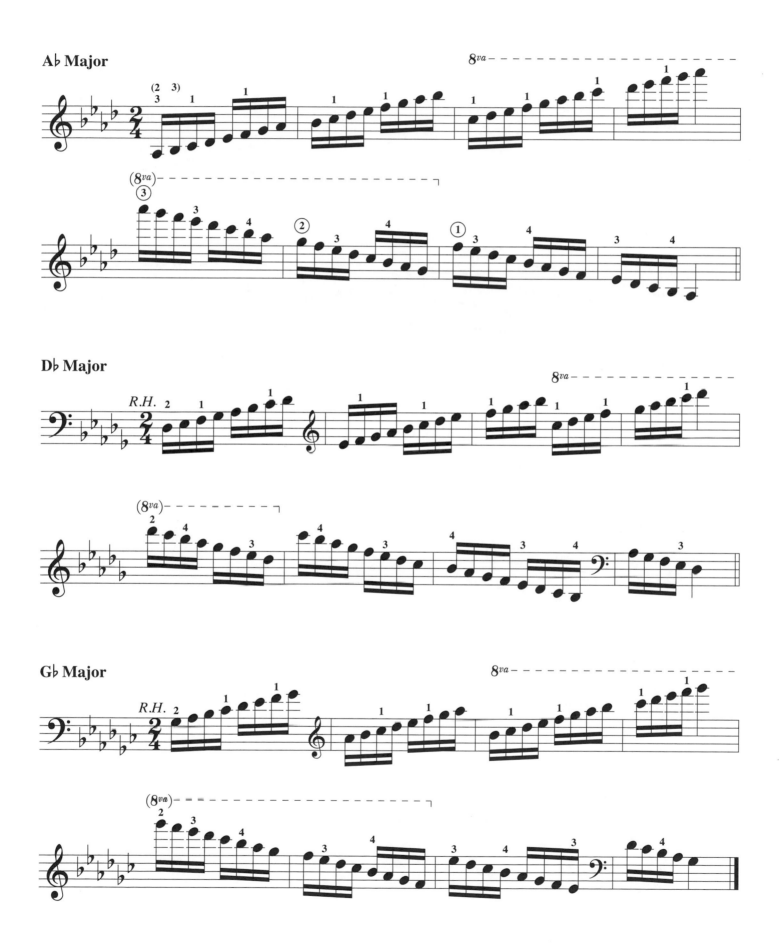

Minor Scales

C Major / A minor

♪ = 100 to ♩ = 80

G Major / E minor

FF302

D Major / B minor

A Major / F♯ minor

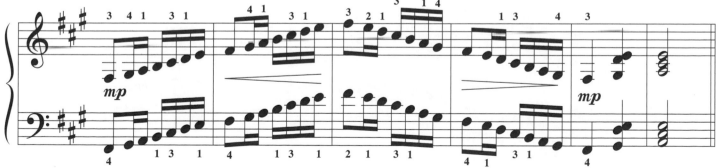

E Major / C♯ minor

B Major / G♯ minor

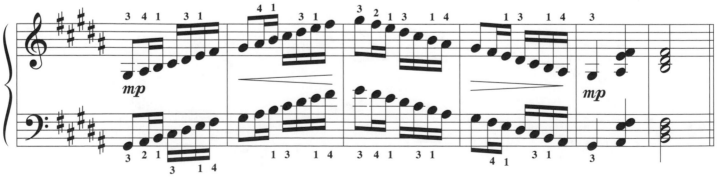

44

F Major / D minor

B♭ Major / G minor

E♭ Major / C minor

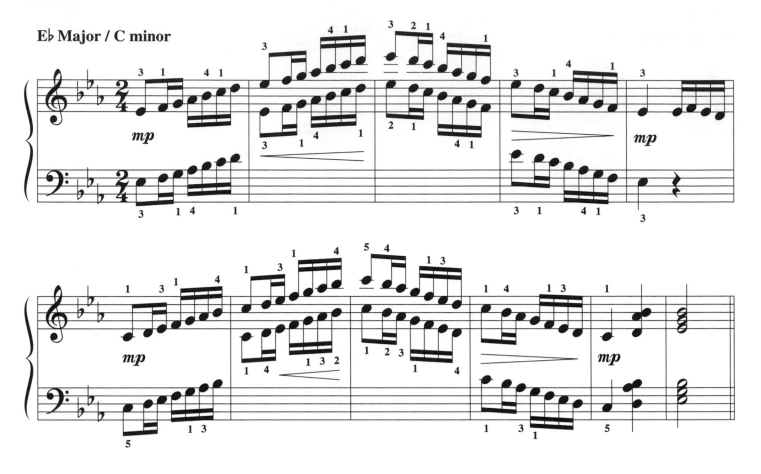

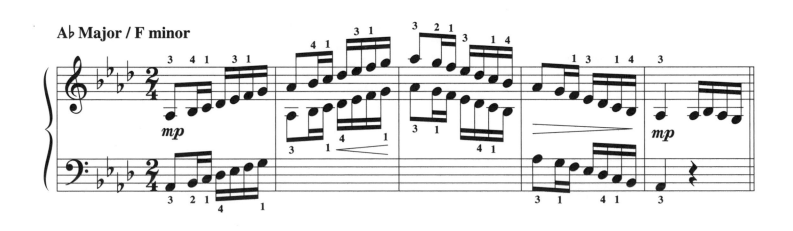

A♭ Major / F minor

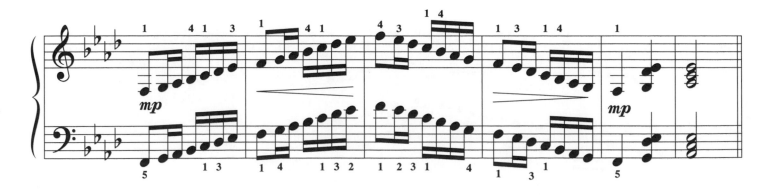

FF302

Db Major / Bb minor

Gb Major / Eb minor

Harmonic Minor Scales

♩ =

72	88	104	120

The previous scales were in *natural minor* form, unchanged from the key signature.

For *harmonic minor* scales, the 7th scale degree is raised to provide a *leading tone*.

A minor

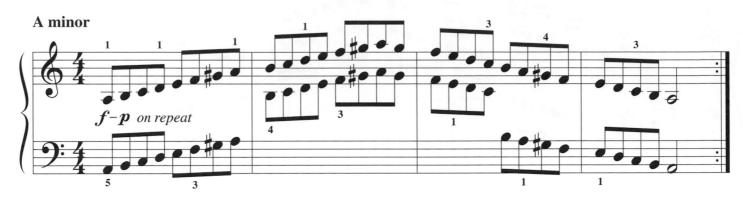

D minor

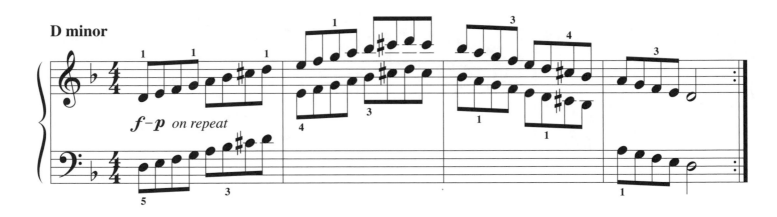

G minor

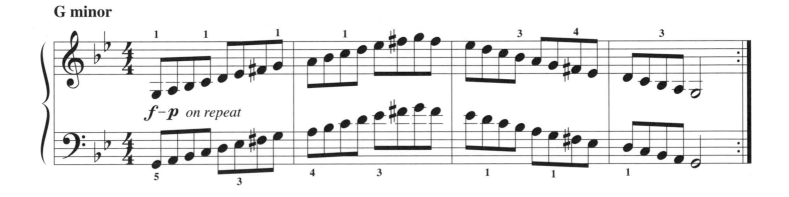

C minor

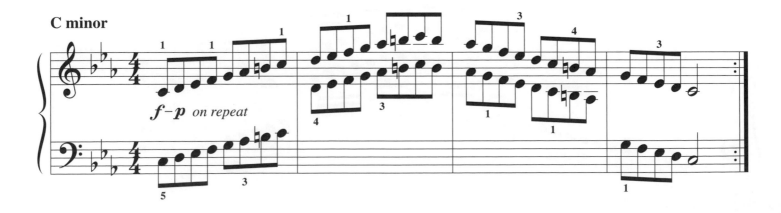

FF302

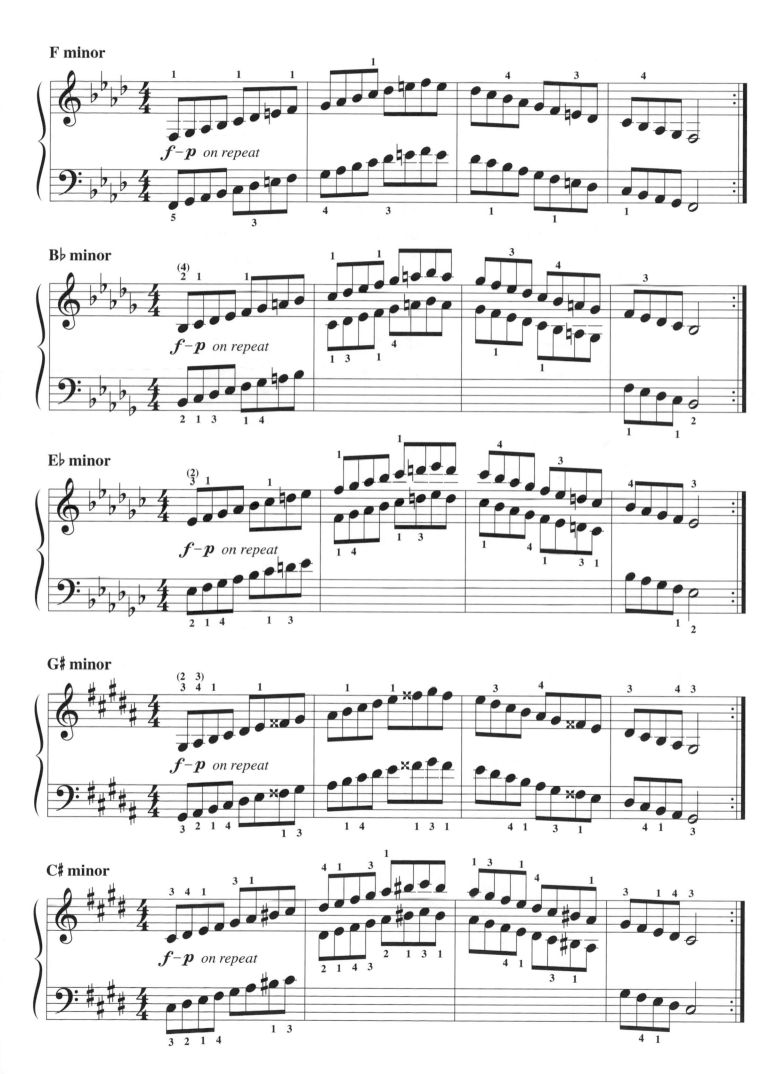

F minor

B♭ minor

E♭ minor

G# minor

C# minor

F# minor

B minor

E minor

Variation: Melodic Minor

For *melodic minor* scales, raise both scale degrees 6 and 7. How does this compare to the major scale?
The natural form of minor (no raised tones) is typically used when descending.

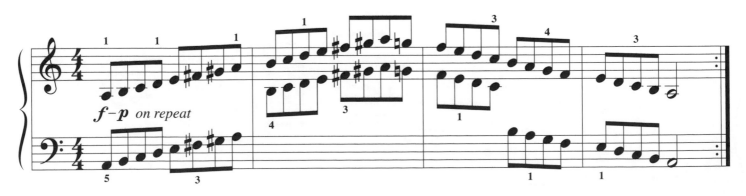

Practice other minor scales in both harmonic and melodic minor forms.

V to I in Minor Keys

Melodic resolution: *leading tone* **to** *tonic*

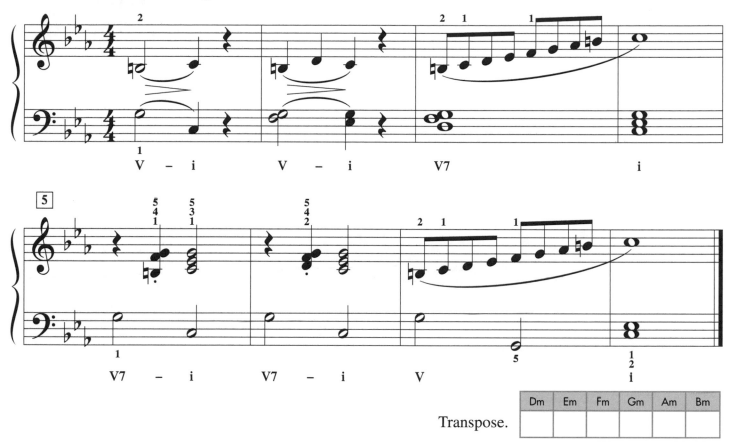

V – i   V – i   V7   i

5

V7 – i   V7 – i   V   i

	Dm	Em	Fm	Gm	Am	Bm
Transpose.						

Melodic resolution: scale degree 2-1

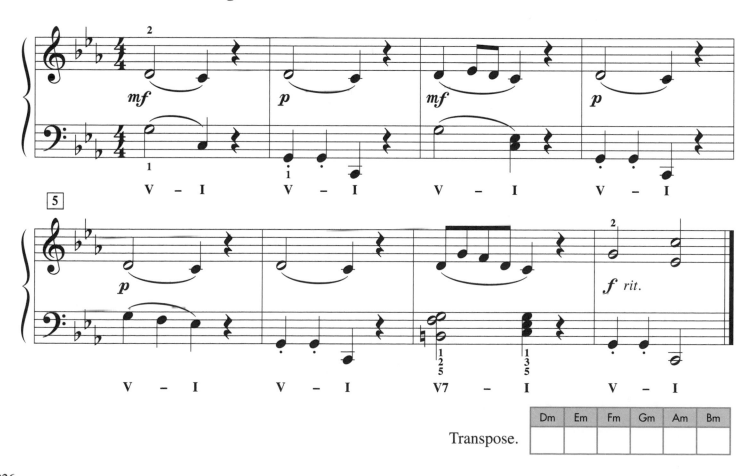

mf   *p*   *mf*   *p*

V – I   V – I   V – I   V – I

5

p   *f* *rit.*

V – I   V – I   V7 – I   V – I

	Dm	Em	Fm	Gm	Am	Bm
Transpose.						

Arpeggios

Wrist Circle Warm-ups

Use an "under and over" motion of the wrist.

Then extend the "swoop under" throughout the L.H. descending arpeggio.

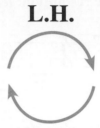

L.H.

Use wrist circles to execute these arpeggios.

FF302

R.H.

Use wrist circles to execute these arpeggios.

Notice the hands move in mirror image.

Use an "under and over" motion of the wrist.

Then extend the "swoop under" throughout the R.H. ascending arpeggio.

Major Arpeggios for L.H.

The opening one-octave arpeggio establishes the "over-and-under" wrist circle for L.H. The multi-octave arpeggio stretches the "swoop over" for the entire ascent and the "swoop under" for the entire descent. When proficient, omit the "warm-up" measure.

Major Arpeggios for R.H.

The opening one-octave arpeggio establishes the "under-and-over" wrist circle for R.H.
The multi-octave arpeggio stretches the "swoop under" for the entire ascent and the
"swoop over" for the entire descent. When proficient, omit the "warm-up" measure.

One-Octave Arpeggio Inversions – Major Chords

Use wrist circles to execute these arpeggiated inversions. Listen for an even tone throughout.

L.H.   **R.H.**

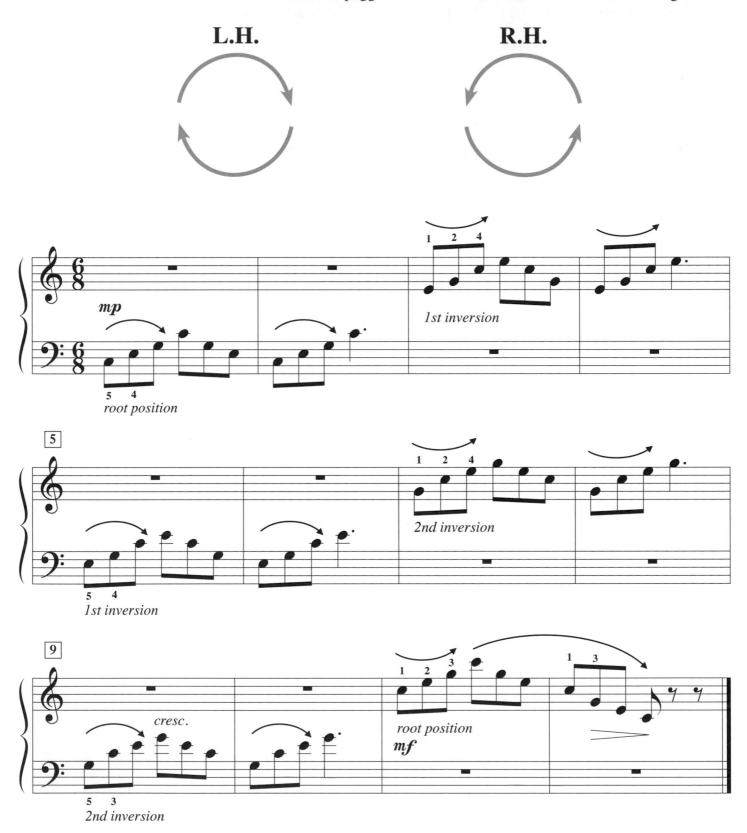

Continue the above exercise in all keys, moving up chromatically.

D♭	D	E♭	E	F	F♯ G♭	G	A♭	A	B♭	B

FF30

Arpeggio Sprints – Major Chords

♩ = 60 to 88

Continue the above exercise on E, F, G, A, and B.

Continue the above exercise on E, F, G, A, and B.

One-Octave Arpeggio Inversions – Minor Chords

Use wrist circles to execute these arpeggiated inversions. Listen for an even tone throughout.

Transpose the above exercise to these keys.

Bm	Cm	Dm	Em	Fm	Gm

Then try on minor chords that begin on black keys.

B♭m	E♭m	G♯m	C♯m	F♯m

Can you work out a fingering
for the last two measures?

Arpeggio Sprints – Minor Chords

♩ = 60 to 88

Continue the above exercise on Cm, Dm, Em, Fm, and Gm.

Continue the above exercise on Cm, Dm, Em, Fm, and Gm.

Major Arpeggios – Extended

Continue the above exercise on F, G, A, and B.

Continue the above exercise on F, G, A, and B.

Minor Arpeggios – Extended

Continue the above exercise on Fm, Gm, Am, and Bm.

Continue the above exercise on Fm, Gm, Am, and Bm.

Flat-Key Arpeggios for L.H.

♩. = 72 to 100

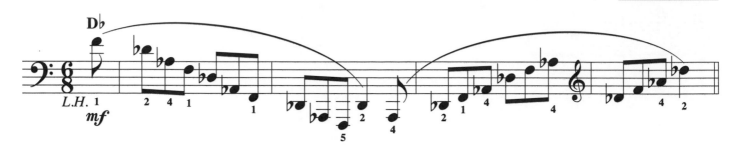

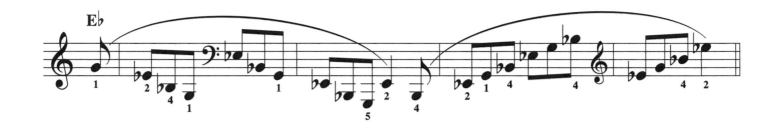

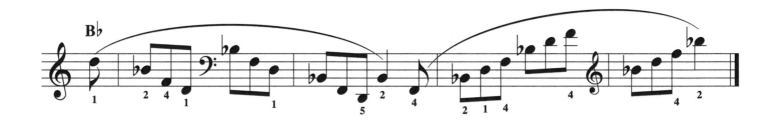

Optional:

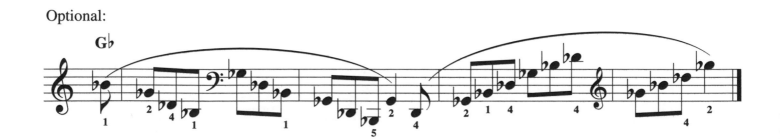

Flat-Key Arpeggios for R.H.

♩. = 88 to 108

Harmony

The basic harmony in a key is derived from chords built on each scale degree.

I, **IV** and **V** chords are *major*; **ii**, **iii**, and **vi** chords are *minor*.

Consider the diminished **vii** chord as the 3rd, 5th and 7th of **V7**. (Also see page 66.)

Here the root movement is "down a 5th." Memorize this important chord pattern.

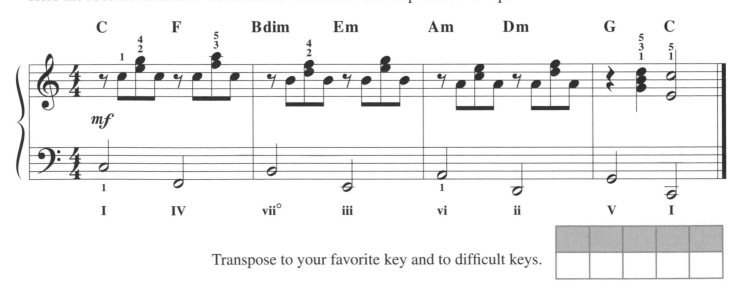

Transpose to your favorite key and to difficult keys.

Chord Function Drills

Write the chord letter names for this common "down a 5th" chord pattern.

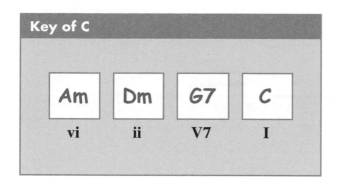

Key of C

Am	Dm	G7	C
vi	ii	V7	I

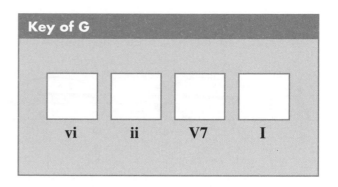

Key of G

vi	ii	V7	I

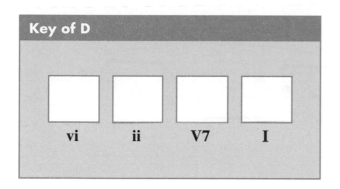

Key of D

vi	ii	V7	I

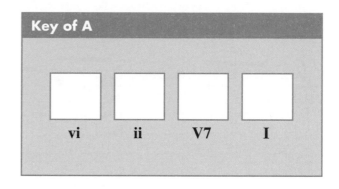

Key of A

vi	ii	V7	I

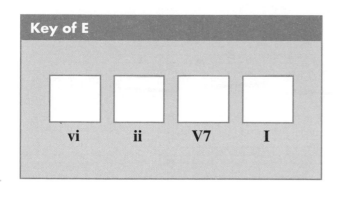

Key of E

vi	ii	V7	I

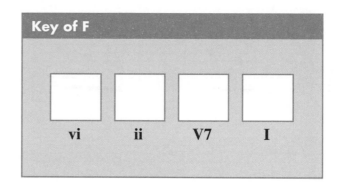

Key of F

vi	ii	V7	I

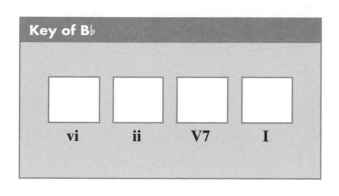

Key of B♭

vi	ii	V7	I

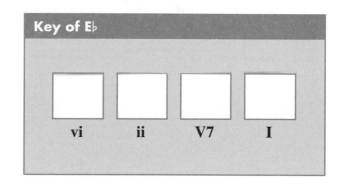

Key of E♭

vi	ii	V7	I

Diatonic Harmony

Diatonic means "through the tonality"; in other words, using notes of the major scale.

Here, the R.H. changes chords over a sustained L.H. bass on the tonic.

Say the chord function as you play and notice whether major or minor.
In measure 7, the vii° chord is harmonized with scale degree 5 in the bass, forming a V7 chord.

Transpose to all keys. For the last measure, use fingers 4-2-1 when playing in flat keys.

G	D	A	E	B	F	B♭	E♭	A♭	D♭	F♯ G♭

FF3C

Chord Progression: I-V7-V7-I

Practice these inversions of I and V7 in many keys.

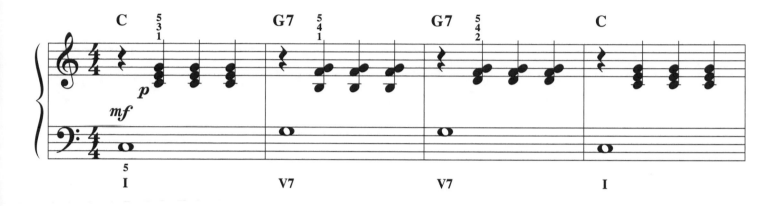

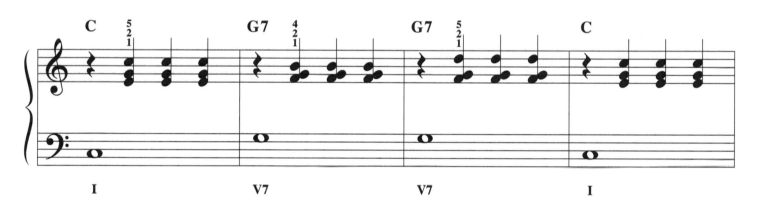

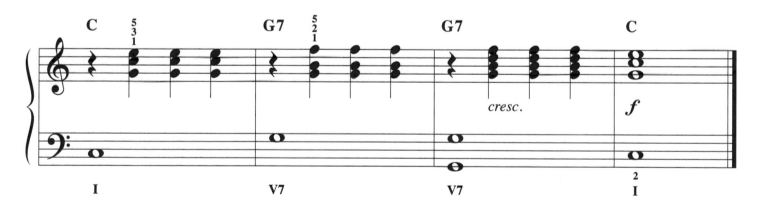

Mark your transposition progress.

C	G	D	A	E	B	F	B♭	E♭	A♭	D♭	F♯/G♭

Chord Progression: I-IV-V7-I

I, **IV** and **V7** chords are played here over a sustained bass note ("pedal point") on the tonic (**I**).

Pedal every two measures, per the harmony changes.

Key of C

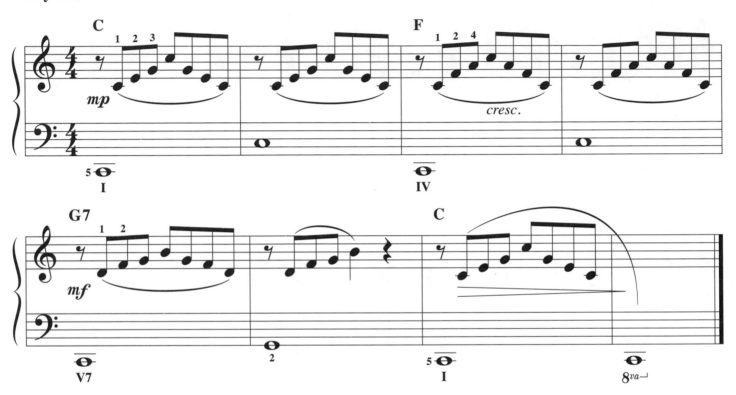

Key of D♭

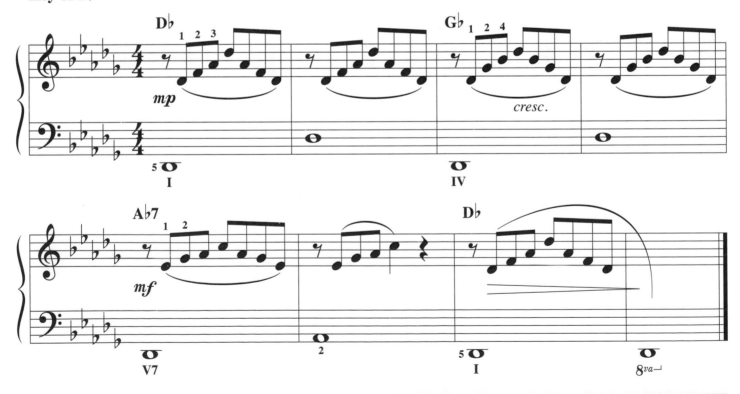

Continue the transposition chromatically through all keys.

D	E♭	E	F	F#/G♭	G	A♭	A	B♭	B

FF30

"Beach Party" Progression: I-vi-IV-V

You may recognize this chord progression as *Heart and Soul,* or as *Beach Party* from the Piano Adventures®
Level 2B Lesson Book. You'll find it in *Stand By Me* and *Runaround Sue* (FunTime® Rock 'n Roll), *My Special Angel*
(BigTime® Rock 'n Roll), and in the introduction to *Morning Has Broken* (BigTime® Favorites). Hear it in recent
chart-toppers such as *Million Reasons* (FunTime® Hits), *All of Me* (BigTime® Hits), and *Perfect* (ChordTime® Hits).

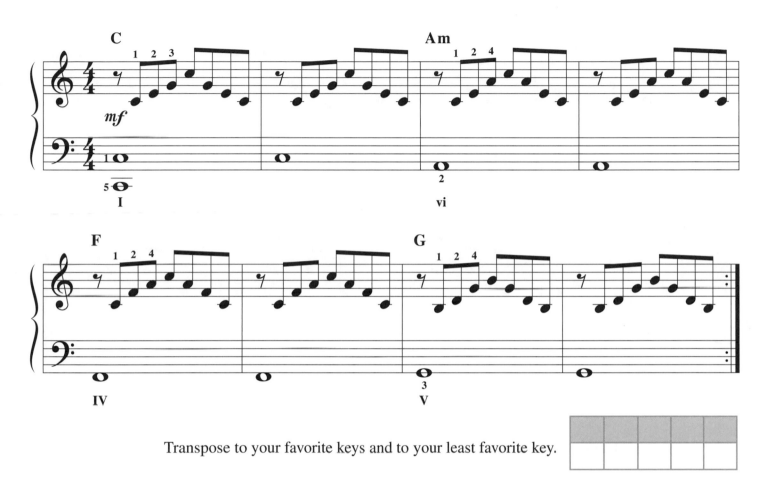

Transpose to your favorite keys and to your least favorite key.

Fill in the boxes with chord names for the following progression.

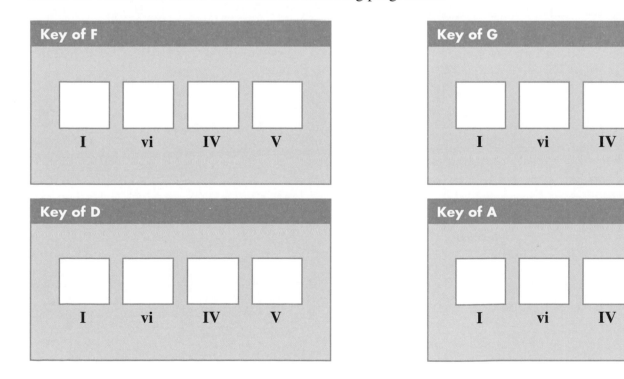

"Pachelbel" Progression: I-V-vi-IV

This chord progression is similar to the *Pachelbel Canon* (BigTime® Classics and BigTime® Popular). You'll find it in the chorus of *Can You Feel the Love Tonight* (BigTime® Kids' Songs), *When a Man Loves a Woman* (BigTime® Rock 'n Roll), and *Someone Like You* (Adult Piano Adventures® Popular Book 1). Hear it in *How Far I'll Go* (ChordTime® Disney) and *Girls Like You* (ShowTime® Hits).

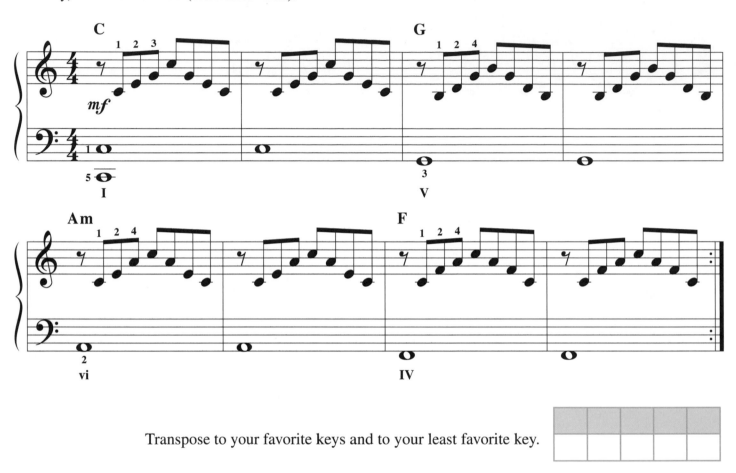

Transpose to your favorite keys and to your least favorite key.

Fill in the boxes with chord names for the following progression.

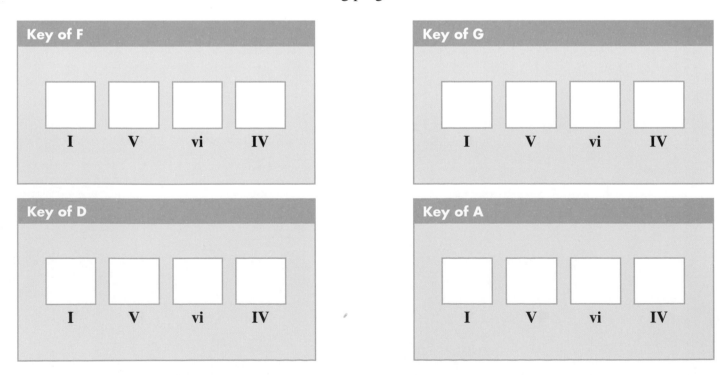

Key of F			
I	V	vi	IV

Key of G			
I	V	vi	IV

Key of D			
I	V	vi	IV

Key of A			
I	V	vi	IV

FF30

"Hip-Hop" Progression: vi-IV-I-V

For a hip-hop or R&B variation, begin on measure 5 of the previous page (vi-IV-I-V).

Then play as shown below.

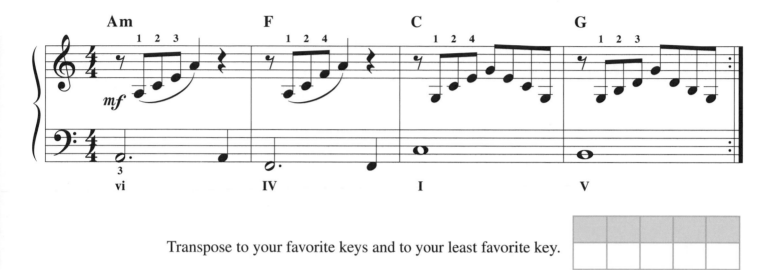

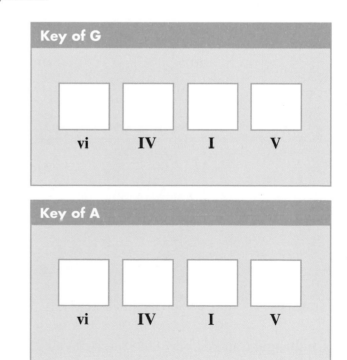

Transpose to your favorite keys and to your least favorite key.

You may have heard this chord progression in Bruno Mars' *Grenade*, Eminem's *Love the Way You Lie*, Timbaland and One Republic's *Apologize*, and many other hip-hop songs (sometimes beginning on the IV chord). Check it out in Sia's dance hit *Cheap Thrills* and the pop ballad *Say Something* by A Great Big World. It is also the chorus of *You Raise Me Up* (BigTime® Popular).

Fill in the boxes with chord names for the following progression.

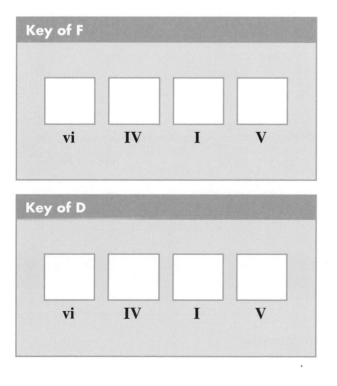

Key of F

vi	IV	I	V

Key of G

vi	IV	I	V

Key of D

vi	IV	I	V

Key of A

vi	IV	I	V

I and V7 in Relative Major and Minor

C Major / A minor

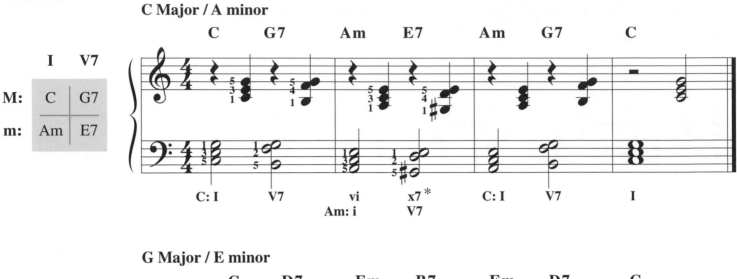

	I	V7
M:	C	G7
m:	Am	E7

G Major / E minor

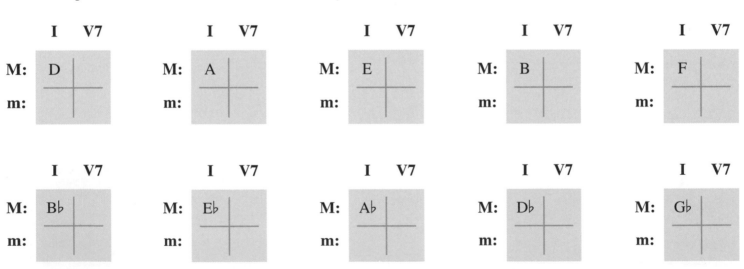

	I	V7
M:	G	D7
m:	Em	B7

Complete each box to indicate I and V7 in major and the relative minor.

	I	V7
M:	D	
m:		

	I	V7
M:	A	
m:		

	I	V7
M:	E	
m:		

	I	V7
M:	B	
m:		

	I	V7
M:	F	
m:		

	I	V7
M:	B♭	
m:		

	I	V7
M:	E♭	
m:		

	I	V7
M:	A♭	
m:		

	I	V7
M:	D♭	
m:		

	I	V7
M:	G♭	
m:		

Transpose the above exercise to all keys.

C	G	D	A	E	B	F	B♭	E♭	A♭	D♭	F♯/G♭

Challenge: Can you play the exercise in all keys going up chromatically?

*x7 is often used to indicate a dominant 7th sound.